Forty Years of Trident Booksellers and Cafe

With contributions by
Hudson Shotwell, James Gimian, Peter Jones, Tyler Lansford, Ian Doreum, Rick Kopp, Evan Colbert, Emily Owens, Emma Gomez, Jenn Zuko, John Lorenz, Santiago Rodríguez Guerro-Strachan, Peter Guarino, Chet Ananda, Mark Kodak, Ben Rietema, Nathaniel Kennon Perkins, Crystal Garcia, & Jethro McClellan

Edited and Designed by
Liz Whitman

TRIDENT PRESS
Boulder, CO

Each piece copyright ©2020 by its respective creator.

Without limiting the rights under copyright, no part of this publication may be reproduced, stored in or introduced into a retrieval system, or transmitted, in any form or by any means (electronic, mechanical, photocopying, recording, or otherwise), without the prior written permission of both the copyright owner and the publisher of this book.

ISBN: 978-1-951226-08-4

Edited and Designed by Liz Whitman

Front Cover Photo by John Lorenz
Back Cover Photo by Andrew Hyde
Cover Layout by Annie Russo

Published by Trident Press/Trident Booksellers and Café
940 Pearl St.
Boulder, CO 80302

tridentcafe.com

Artwork by Mark Inman

the Trident's
a solid space

is it some   quasi-

    ethereal

"temple of golden grace"?

maybe.

it need not be.

it is

silver

and

merely

a hugely holy place

from each brick

in
old
wall

a face
from Trident's past

(gone-by-infinitely-　　　*slowly/*

infinitelyfast)

40 years

appears,

looks out at the space,

blesses this

now and e'er

holy

place

Poems by: Jethro McClellan

The Early Days

The Birth of an Icon

On a cold, winter day in 1979 just after the Christmas holiday, Hudson Shotwell and James Gimian sat down to sign some papers and realize a dream. Both men worked in books and publishing, and both loved coffee. They had long dreamed of opening their own bookstore and cafe in the heart of Boulder.

James Gimian started his career in bookselling by founding the Seed Center Bookstore in Palo Alto in 1972, which became locally famous and a new center of counterculture by (re)publishing Thaddeus Golas' *The Lazy Man's Guide to Enlightenment* (1971), the Bible of California-style spirituality. Eventually, Gimian joined Shambhala Publications on Telegraph Avenue in Berkeley. When Shambhala Publications moved to Boulder in 1976, Gimian came along as Vice President. Gimian had long hoped to own a business of his own in Boulder, and one day in 1979 when walking down Pearl Street he saw a for lease sign in the window of 940 Pearl. The space was perfect! Gimian pitched the idea of a bookstore to his good friend Hudson Shotwell, and they got to work, signing papers and incorporating the Trident on December 29, 1979.

All winter and for the rest of spring Gimian continued to work at Shambhala Publications, and would come in to the store on his lunch breaks and after work while Hudson worked day by day constructing the bookshelves and fixtures. Finally, on June 1st of 1980, Trident Booksellers officially opened for business. All summer long crowds would browse the bookstore shelves for great deals on quality new, used, and remainder books. But something still was missing, and soon Gimian and Shotwell would add one more feature that would turn Trident into an icon.

Hudson Shotwell and James Gimian outside of 940 Pearl St

Left: Hudson Shotwell / Right: James Gimian

Don't torch books

Editor:

Wait! Don't burn those metaphysical books! Contrary to the Pentacostal whatsit, we at Trident Booksellers have a better idea. Sell your new age books to us (since we can barely keep them in stock as it is). We will give you cold, hard cash and sell them to other people, collecting sales tax in a dutiful manner, which will be mailed to the City of Boulder, thereby enabling said city to pick up the general trash in the spring, including the ashes from whatever else the Pentacostal whatsit burns next week.

Pretty good deal, huh?

HUDSON B. SHOTWELL
940 Pearl St.

Coffee Comes to Books

In 1980, Boulder - let alone most of the United States - didn't have any espresso bars, and Shotwell and Hudson both missed the old school lattes they would have at Café Mediterranean on Telegraph Avenue in Berkley back in the late 1970s. They always had hoped to include a coffee counter in the bookstore, so a year later when the space next door became available, they rented that space as well, and opened up part of the pine wood walls that separated the spaces. They expanded the bookstore to include the back half of the new space, and constructed a coffee counter, dish area, and a half-wall in the front for a European style café. Shotwell and Gimian traveled back to Berkley to source equipment for the café. They ordered the same type of espresso machine as their favorite café had, a bright orange Rancilio, along with the same drip coffee machine that the original Pete's Coffee by UC Berkley used. They had beans imported from an Italian company out of San Francisco. Hudson was taught how to pull espresso and foam milk by Sam Bercholz, owner of Shambhala Publications. After some practice - and a lot of bad lattés - they officially opened the café, and Trident Booksellers and Café as it is known today was born.

According to Hudson, "The first time I knew we had the real goods was when a women came in and ordered a single cappuccino. I pulled the shot and steamed the milk as Sam had shown me, then handed it over the little granite countertop. She was the only customer that morning. She took it over to the table by the east window. I surreptitiously watched her take her first sip. She did, then closed her eyes and gave a big sigh. We had lift off." To this day, 40 years later, that little granite countertop continues to pump out some of the best coffee, tea, and espresso in the United States.

Above: Barista serving up something good / Below: Amy Tvetne working the counter

Some cool cats hanging out front

John Bizarro, owner of John's resturants

Left: Tyler Lansford / Right: Douglas Arbuthnot circa 1983

■ TRIDENT'S HAZE CLEARS: Boulder's Trident Cafe has always had a special urban air about it, an ambiance that evokes the fine, hip coffee hang-outs of Boston and San Francisco. It has always been a scene seen through a murky purple haze of imported cigarette smoke. One could stop by for a serious cup of coffee, a serious intellectual conversation and an exhilarating lungful or two of secondary smog.

However, even the Trident has cleaned up its act or at least its air. A high-tech, air-exchange ventilation system has been installed and the front section of the cafe is now non-smoking. The number of non-smoking seats has also been increased. Although there had been complaints from bookstore habitues, the clincher, says Trident owner Hudson Shotwell, was that he was tired of going home at night with his undershirts smelling like an ashtray.

We hope the rare air of existential ennui is not impaired as a result of the change.

Daily Camera - January 25, 1989

Non-coffee achiever to take cafe complaint to City Council

By DIANE EASTRIDGE
Colorado Daily Staff Writer

Steve Martinot believes that he is being discriminated against because he does not like tea and prefers not to drink coffee in the afternoon. He plans to ask the City Council tonight to do something about it.

Martinot said he likes to go to the Trident cafe and bookstore, at 940 Pearl St., to buy books and to "mingle in a relaxed atmosphere," as a break from the writing he does at home. The sort of atmosphere and conversation for which the place is known stimulates opinions and helps keep the town vital, he says. But about two weeks ago, Martinot was barred from the cafe because he takes up space without buying a cup of the Trident's locally famous Java.

Hudson Shotwell, the owner of the cafe, said he has nothing against Martinot, but that the high volume of business at the coffeehouse during the winter months prohibits the management from allowing people to go in and just hang out. He said Martinot is just one of many who have been asked to leave for similar reasons.

Boulder's trespassing code grants establishment owners or managers the right to exclude anyone from their premises. Martinot believes that power has been used to keep him from the cultural experience of "hanging out with friends and engendering an on-going dialogue."

"My disagreement with the management of the Trident arises from the fact that I don't drink tea, never having found a tea that agrees with me; I tend to stay away from sweet foods such as soda, fruit juices, and cake; and I often feel that drinking coffee through the afternoon is detrimental to my stomach," Martinot wrote, asking the council to change the trespassing code.

While Martinot said he usually stays at the cafe for short periods of time, he acknowledged he does stay for long conversations with friends "every now and then."

At tonight's meeting, Martinot plans to ask the council to consider changing the city's trespassing guidelines, making it unlawful to expel a person who has not committed an "overt act," from unhosted establishments.

Colorado Daily - 1987

■ **THE RIGHT-TO-DAWDLE MOVEMENT:** From our Only-In-Boulder department comes the potentially ground-breaking complaint by resident Steve Martinot. Martinot was barred from The Trident Cafe by owner Hudson Shotwell because of his penchant for visiting to talk, without buying coffee, muffins or books at the establishment. It seems like a reasonable action for a business owner. Martinot wrote to the Boulder City Council urging it to amend local trespassing statutes which are used to prevent him from "hanging out with friends and engendering an on-going dialogue." He wrote that he would like to buy something at the cafe, but he doesn't prefer the coffee, tea, soda or foods offered there. Things are rough all over, eh?

I can sort of relate, though. After all these past exciting decades of having to do things, go places and be things, perhaps we are ready for a few years of stay-at-home D&V: Domestication and Vegetation. We wonder whether this cafe-society born "Right-To-Dawdle" movement could be a public manifestation of the domestic couch potato trend, which prognosticators say will sweep the nation in '88. Nuke a TV dinner and stay tuned.

Daily Camera - Johnn Lehndorff - 1987

Charlie Johnson/Colorado Daily

BEST PLACE TO PLAY A PICK-UP GAME OF CHESS

☛ TRIDENT CAFE

Dog Day Afternoon Award

By what standards does one measure a coffee house? Most obvious, perhaps, is the very quality of the coffee itself. Of course, it takes more than a lukewarm cup of joe to a coffee house make; the best java huts of Boulder are popular for their ambience, attitude and animal-magnetism. That is, the animals that are magnetically attracted to their early-morning, mid-morning, late-morning, early-afternoon, mid-afternoon, etc... cups of decaf double half & half. This year's Annual People's Choice Award Winner for Best Coffee House is no exception. The **Trident Cafe** is Boulder's downtown headquarters for the mug-seeking masses of Boulder County.

THANK YOU BOULDER FOR OUR FIRST 10 YEARS —

TRIDENT BOOKSELLERS INC.

ANNIVERSARY SALE

10% OFF ALL BOOKS AND CARDS
SATURDAY, JUNE 9, 10 am - 11 pm

940 PEARL ST.　　(coffee not included)　　443-3133

Espresso	A straight shot of dark roast coffee, extracted by steam.	.90
Doppio Espresso	Twice the amount and punch as the above.	1.50
Cappuccino	A shot of espresso served with steamed milk and hot, frothy foam. Delicioso!	1.35
Makkiotto	Same as cappuccino, but served in a mug with a little more hot milk.	1.50
Café Latte	Double shot of espresso, served in a 16 oz. glass with hot, foamy steamed milk. Famous at the Café Med in Berkeley and famous here.	1.85
Café au Lait	In a bowl or large glass, Trident Blend coffee served with hot, foamy milk.	1.40
Cappuccino Orzata	Cappuccino with a shot of sweet almond syrup.	1.60
Café Mocha	Served in a mug, espresso and chocolate with steamed milk, topped with fresh whipped cream made by our own Hungarian contraption. Very tasty & delightful.	1.75
Hot Chocolate Florentine	In a large glass, our delicious house coffee mixed with foamy hot chocolate.	1.55
Decaf Espresso versions of the above	We use Swiss water-processed decaffeinated beans.	+ .25

These drinks are topped with your choice of cocoa, cinnamon, or nutmeg.

• • •

Trident Coffee (With one refill)	Our house coffee is blended and roasted here in town. Strong, but not bitter, you are assured of a freshly brewed cup.	.75
	Each refill after the first:	.35
Small Coffee To Go	You may serve yourself (no refill).	.55
Large Coffee To Go	You may serve yourself (no refill).	.75
Decaffeinated Drip Coffee	(Swiss water processed) With one refill.	.75 .95
Small Decaf To Go	(No refill)	.60
Large Decaf To Go	(No refill)	.95

Hot Chocolate	A mug of hot chocolate, rich and foamy.	1.10
Hot Chocolate with Whipped Cream	Make whipped cream, not war.	1.25

"Ask for hot chocolate drinks made not-so-hot for children."

• • •

TEAS

Pot for One	We preheat the pot!	.75
Pot for Two	Two bags in a larger pot.	1.25

    English Breakfast   Black Current   Almond Sunset
    Ceylon Breakfast   Cinnamon Rose   Spearmint
    Irish Breakfast   Peppermint   Emperor's Choice
    Earl Grey   Sleepytime
    Prince of Wales   Red Zinger

Il Hwa XXX Ginseng	Cold processed tea from Korea. Two packet pot	.85 1.50

• • •

Hansen's Juices	Apple or Apple-Strawberry, in bottles. With or without ice?	.95
Milk	Milk from regional cows.	.70

PASTRIES

	Would you like butter with your pastry?	
Muffins	Homemade muffins baked in the Rocky Mountains!	1.15
Croissants	Brought to Venice by Turkish invaders in the Middle Ages, now available to us.	.95
Danish	Cherry, Blueberry, etc., with cream cheese.	.95
Other	Please ask.	market

Trident Menu circa 1980's

COLD DRINKS Year round availability.

Italian Sodas Like phosphates of the old days, we bring our syrups to you from the coast of California! A jigger of syrup over ice stirred with fizzy water. .95

Vanilla • Cherry • Strawberry • Blackberry • Lemon • Orgeat
Kiwi • Apricot • Raspberry • Tamarindo • Lime • Cranberry

Carbonated Water On ice, we filter the particulates. .70

Well Sodas 16 oz. glass of Coke, Ginger Ale, or Cherry 7-Up. .75

SUMMER DRINKS

Iced Coffee Cold house coffee poured over ice. With milk? .95

Iced Cappuccino Hot weather relief! Cold espresso over ice, with cool milk, topped with foamy milk. 1.85

Iced Mocha An iced cappuccino with chocolate added. 2.00

Iced Tea Orange Pekoe with one refill. .75

Iced Herbal Tea Flavors vary, please ask. (No refill) .80

•   •   •

The Trident Café has been serving fine coffees since 1982. Your continued patronage, support and patience have allowed us to grow and expand our hours into the evenings. We are pleased to announce that we are now open evenings until eleven in both the café and bookstore. We appreciate your business!

TRIDENT CAFÉ

940 PEARL STREET
BOULDER, COLORADO

The Sunday Camera - October 24, 1982

Photos by Charles Wendt

They Come For Coffee And Words

By Donna Joy Newman

A month ago, Justina Hayden came to Boulder from Napa Valley, Calif., to spend eight months in this area taking outdoor leadership training and, on the side, learning computer programming.

Soon she was exploring the Downtown Mall in her spare time and discovered the Trident Booksellers and Cafe at 940 Pearl St.

It was like a homecoming. "I owned a bookstore in Calistoga (Calif.) and I had a coffee shop in it too," said the 42-year-old woman one morning last week. Spread out next to her coffee cup on the table at the cafe was a loose-leaf notebook of computer lessons.

Hayden's Pearl Street discovery — a place where long conversations mingle compatibly with the coffee — is a phenomenon of long-standing tradition in Europe and well known in recent years to inhabitants of the East and West Coasts and in such cities as Chicago.

It's finally taking Boulder by storm, and many coffeehouse patrons wonder why it didn't hit sooner, so natural is it for a sophisticated city where people have a lot to say to each other.

As recently as a couple of years ago, you could hardly find a good cup of espresso in Boulder. Now there are a dozen or more places that serve it, most of them fitting the coffeehouse mold, and most of them started within the last couple of years.

The ambience ranges from old-world cozy to modern hi-tech. But whether they're called coffeehouse, espresso salon, espresso bar, or cafe, they have certain characteristics in common.

They serve espresso and a wide range of other European coffee concoctions, croissants and other fine breads and pastries. Some offer wine and beer as well. Several also serve nice lunches of the salad-sandwich-quiche variety and a couple get even more elaborate than that, with the likes of pierogis, Wellingtons or pates on the menu. Some also offer wine and/or beer.

A customer may just drop in for a quick carry-out coffee and Danish in the morning, but that's missing the point of coffeehouses. Like the cafes of the Parisian Left Bank, they're places to linger, talk trivia or deep thoughts, people-watch, read, think, or meditate.

Trident co-owner and manager Hudson Shotwell said the combination book and coffee shop concept originated about five years ago in Washington, D.C., and is even being marketed in franchise form by a company called Upstart Crow in California.

"It's like the bookstore is the linear part and the coffee shop is the reading between the lines."

The Brillig Bookshop on the Hill, established in 1965, was the first combination shop, having added its Tearoom two years ago.

Both Trident and Brillig have the inviting atmosphere of old wooden floors (and exposed brick walls at the Trident). It's not unusual for habitues to take a book from a shelf and settle in for an hour or two at a table. For regular patrons, these and other coffeehouses are social meeting places that frequently inspire deep impromptu discussions. They also go to the Brillig for poetry readings and musical performances.

TALK AT THE TRIDENT
Diana Janezic, assistant manager of The Ritz in Boulder, and Gary Purchase, a landscaper, go to the Trident Cafe on Pearl Street, right, nearly every weekday morning to drink coffee and talk. They think it has just about the best coffee in Boulder and they like being able to browse among the books.

The Sunday Camera - November 1, 1987

Time out of time at the Trident

"Poet or ploughman, statesman or derelict — everyman has his Mermaid's Tavern, every hamlet its shrine to conviviality, and in the image of the common spirit of those who haunt it, the character of the shrine is fashioned."

— From "West With the Night," by Beryl Markham

By KAREN TELLEEN

Fountain pens are very much in vogue at the Trident Cafe. There, you can watch them glide gracefully across notebook pages, wielded by authors who look wistful, as if writing odes.

Such a pastime would fit in perfectly at the Trident, a space that, when he first saw it eight years ago, reminded one of its owners of England and of the sea. There is no decor, simply ambiance.

The cafe occupies the western half of a building shared with Trident Booksellers, where many customers procure their reading materials. Satisfied with their selections, they settle into booths or chairs, often sipping a cappucino while devouring words.

A late-autumn afternoon. The cafe is crowded. The glass-paned door opens and closes frequently to usher in new arrivals with a rush of fresh fall air that dissipates even more quickly than it comes in.

The Trident is filled with gentle sounds. White china clinks as cups and saucers are placed on the serving counter; the wooden floor creaks in response to the assaults of jogging, hiking or walking shoes; a harpsichord is filtered through the speakers, offering up a little Bach as a background melody.

In here, time's ebb and flow seems irrelevant. You can still, if you wish hard enough, make time stop."

Seated in a corner near the front door is a solitary young woman who clutches a golden-titled paperback version of "Lolita." She reads precious little of the text, preferring to focus her gaze somewhere beyond the window, over private horizons. Now and then she puffs on a long, slender cigarette, expelling the smoke in slow-moving currents.

The real action is in center ring, at a table of five. The clear leader of the pack here is a lanky guy with sharp features and a bandana around his head. Pale reddish hair trickles down to his shoulders, where it falls listlessly on an old army jacket. He is building an argument with a woman in a red sweater who sits across from him. They bandy back and forth; the words "respect" and "disrespect" are exchanged more than once, like weapons.

The leader prepares to strut out, surrounded by his remaining three devotees: two rather nondescript followers and a tall boy with a hint of a moustache on a chiseled, angelic face. He is a black-leathered version of Thomas Gainsborough's "Blue Boy."

The woman in the red sweater remains alone at the table. She removes a compact from her purse. Peering into its depths as if looking for answers, she smoothes the makeup on her cheek. The last glimpse of her as she finally leaves, is of the back of a black leather jacket, with a pair of silver handcuffs festooned from the belt loops.

Inside the Cafe, Jack Kerouac surveys the scene from a poster advertising a conference in his name held in 1982, the same year the Trident opened. At the Trident, Kerou-

Continued on page 5

ac's name is often invoked by those who have never read him, as well as by the cognoscenti. Here, the Beat Generation, the hippies, the radicals of the past are all conversationally exhumed by people born after the fact. These people emulate a perceived mentality, a style, ignorant of the nuance.

Trident regulars routinely stroll through the cafe with cups or teapots in hand, returning unabashedly to the counter for refills.

The 5 o'clock line grows, the chairs fill up with fresh recruits.

A comfortably seated foursome, two men and two women, all with hairdos of identical color and length, discusses various aspects of Buddhism.

"The world is an illusion ... you have to relate to something more pure," says one, while another sucks gently on a plum.

"Certain actions have consequences," continues another.

The ceiling fans turn slowly until 8 p.m., when Bach is replaced by a soft, mellow jazz. In the half-filled cafe, a woman in aqua rolls her cigarette from a pouch of Drum tobacco while reading Jane Austen.

A few feet away, another woman studies Fielding's "History of Tom Jones," and drags on a commercial cigarette.

The two employees behind the counter mull over the strong and weak points of a restaurant in Paris, covering the kitchen floor plan before moving on to a discussion of the French attitude toward foreigners.

The spacious back room, with its newly installed booths, resembles the waiting room of an old train station. Three men sit against the wall, each separated from the next by a full table's length. They all read, lifting their cups to their lips without breaking stride, as if practicing an ancient meditative art form known only to them.

Outside, the night conducts itself in the ordinary way, darkness punctuated by sounds of people who want merely to come or go. In here, time's ebb and flow seems irrelevant. You can still, if you wish hard enough, make time stop. ∎

KAREN TELLEEN, a Boulder writer, is a frequent contributor to The Sunday Camera Magazine.

"Here, the Beat Generation, the hippies, the radicals of the past are all conversationally exhumed by people born after the fact."

The Trident Booksellers and Cafe by Ian Doreum

The following peiece was written for a enviromental design course (ENVD 275) at CU Boulder in 1985.

There is a place for most human customs. The more popular customs have something to do with replenishing the body. The most common example of this is a restaurant. People go to restaurants to socialize, to go out, and to fill their stomachs. Another example is a tavern or bar. This is a place where one is welcome, recognized, can relax and can get a buzz (if desired). A third type of setting is the cafe or coffee house. In contrast to a restaurant or bar which are dark and relaxing, most coffee houses are lit-up and full of energy. The Trident Bookstore and Café is no exception. It is a place where a person can go to get intellectually stimulated.

There are three factors contributing to this stimulation. First, there is a lot of good coffee and pastries. This isn't a very good place to get a meal—just enough sugar and caffeine to get your mind running off in five different directions at once. Second, in the adjoining space there are hundreds of used and out of date books, covering just about any topic. Also there is a rack of newspapers, nothing but the most intellectual: the Chicago Tribune, the New York Times, and the Wall Street Journal to mention a few. The only other place that I know of where one can find this sort of reading is in the public library.

The final condition is the atmosphere. People are reading, conducting business, discussing an idea – things are happening. It isn't a place where one would want to take a nap. Contributing to this atmosphere is the layout of the cafe. Its design is based on self-sufficiency. If you want something you get up and get it, otherwise you will be left alone. Besides being left alone by the waitresses – the cafe is well lit, well ventilated, and has an uncluttered arrangement. All of these combine to make a great place to read.

The Trident Booksellers and Café was named after the mythological three pronged spear. The spear's prongs are used to cut out ignorance, aggression and passion. The creators of this cafe/bookstore wanted it to be a place of thought and reason. Everybody is on the same level; it isn't a place to flaunt one's dispositions – there is curiosity without any stigma.

TRIDENT

When entering the cafe, one notices that even though the building's facade faces north, the entire wall is made of framed glass and is shaded by a canvas awning. If I didn't know better, I would have assumed that the building just swung around 180 degrees. It is the only store front on the south side of the street that has an awning. These large windows bring in the soft northern light, which is very appealing (if heating isn't a factor). The entrance is built about three feet in, which seems common with restored turn-of-the-century buildings. This creates a space on either side for plants – like a box window. The wood floor is old, scuffed, and squeaky when stepped on. A man walks in and leaves the door open – nobody really notices. There are little round wooden tables, each can seat two people, though there is one person to a table now. The chairs are oval, classical-hotel-type, with purple vinyl that matches the paint on the inside of the window frame (how aristocratic). A man wearing an old purple sweatshirt and sand colored corduroy overalls is reading a paper, intently, in one hand while a cigarette burns away in the other. Another man comes in with torn up tennis-shoes, granny glasses, and a day old beard. A lady sits in the corner wearing old jeans, a purple east Indian pull over, and a light weight blue thermal shirt; she looks relaxed drinking her tea. The layout of the cafe is cubic and utilitarian. There is a real urban quality to the cafe, it wouldn't be out of place if it were built in Manhattan.

After choosing what coffee I will have at the counter, wondering what all the coffee contraptions do, and looking at all the pastries in a glass and oak display case, I noticed that there is a quieter space behind the partition at the end of the counter. This area is like a gallery, there are black and white photographs framed and mounted into the raw brick wall. The pictures circle three-quarters of the way around the space all at eye level. The floor is still dotted with round tables and purple chairs. This area is set aside for non-smokers. A bus-person brought fresh purple flowers to my table in a miniature karaf. She looks gypsy-ish with long loose dress and sandals.

Along the west wall of the gallery is a wood stove with a metal guard around it. This would be a good spot to warm up on a snowy day. There are people discussing heavy topics, and walking around in stocking feet. As I look out beyond the people, out the back windows, I can see Canyon Blvd. Above the tall southward windows is a long slopping over-hang that would keep out any direct sunlight even during the winter solstice. On the east side is a unisex bathroom beside a storage room.

Both are contained in a white box framed room, which is shaped the same as the cafe. The ceiling of the storage room/bathroom is only eight feet high. This creates a space to throw up empty boxes – since the ceiling of the cafe is about twelve feet high. North of the bathroom is the opening to the bookstore. The opening is big enough that the most noticeable sign of transition was a bump on the floor. On the wall next to this opening is the newspaper rack, a Buddhist poster and a sign that tells customers to not do homework in the cafe when it is busy.

What really makes this a nice atmosphere is its sounds and smells. Instead of mindless commercial radio, there is a jazz recording filling spaces between conversation and whirrs of espresso machines. The cafe smells of fresh coffee, incense and smoke. I can notice the smoke, but it isn't offensive. There is a cool breeze coming from the ceiling – three large fans keep the air fresh.

After finishing my coffee, I wonder into the bookshop. It feels more like I am walking through someone's house than a store – there is no obnoxious commercialism. In the bookstore all the walls are lines with books up to about six and a half feet high, everything can be reached without a ladder. The categories start with parenting and sexuality, and end with religion, mystery and mysticism at the back of the store. The anxiety one usually feels about looking through, and damaging, virgin books is gone. All of the books in this store have been read, looked over, and contemplated. There is no problem with just looking around. The person behind the counter is sorting through books and answering a customer's questions. There is nothing uncomfortable about the bookstore. The sales counter is at waist level, just the right height to set down books or to scribble down an ISBN number.

The bookstore was started in 1980 as a business venture between two people who had an interest in old books. After three years, the bookstore wasn't going as well as intended. The co-owners cut a hole in their westward wall and built a cafe in the next room. At first the cafe had books in the "gallery" section. After a while books started to get damaged, and the cafe was getting busier – the books where moved back to just the bookstore. The popular cafe now keeps both businesses above water.

The music and commotion of the cafe filter into the bookstore. The literature and intellect of the bookstore filter into the cafe. Both compliment each other, one wouldn't be the same without the other. That is what makes the Trident Booksellers and Café such a unique place.

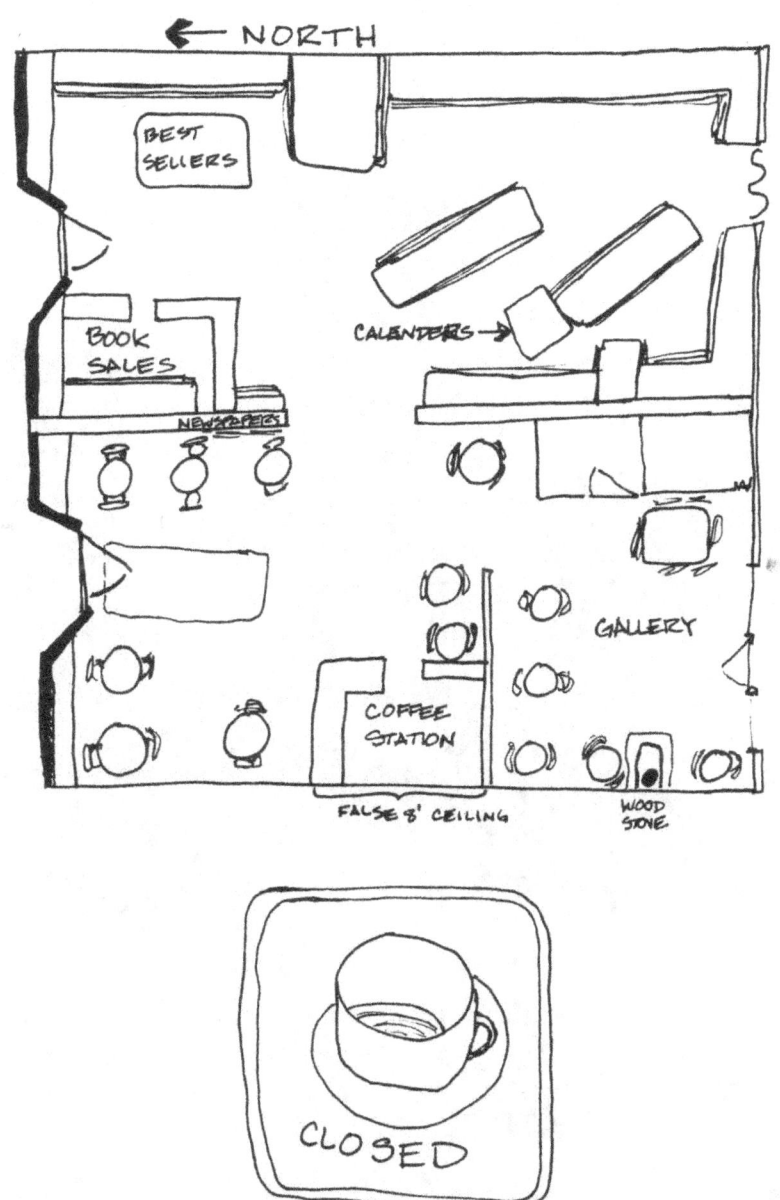

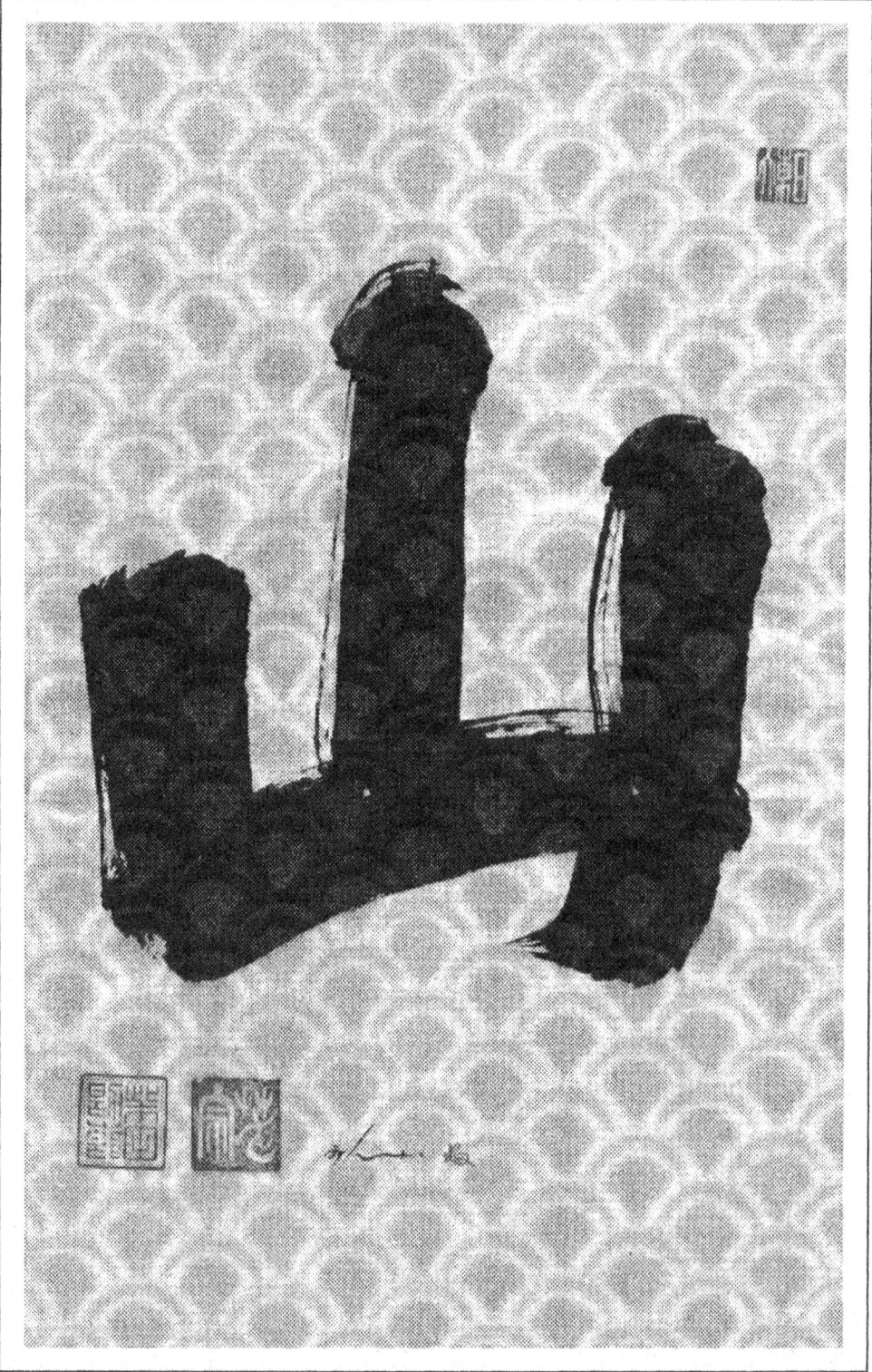

The Trident Symbol

The three pronged Trident logo is the Chinese shan symbol meaning mountain. The symbol used by Trident was painted by Chogyam Trungpa Rinpoche for the Kasung, the military branch of Shambhala. The motto of the Kasung is "Victory over War". War represents the struggle created by the three "poisons" identified by the Buddha: ignorance, aggresion and passion. Victory is meeting these poisons with insight and loving kindness. Mike Smith, being part of the original Kasung, was granted permission to use the Japanese Sumi-E styled trident painted by Trungpa for the store. The Trident still adheres to these principles - waging a war of loving kindess against ignorance, aggression and passion.

An Icon Becomes A Legacy

The 1990s and 2000s were good to Trident - we found our calling - serving the greater community with loving kindness. Mike Smith, the manager during these years, ran a tight ship. He was a hawk about the coffee, passionate about tea, and a lover of books. Yet beyond that, Mike was a people person - he cared about each and every employee and customer in a deep, personal way. That compassion, that dedication, that service is what set Trident apart and allowed us to flourish. Numerous other cafes and bookstores came and went - some even being so bold as to open directly across the street. Yet none of them lasted. The community knew where to put their dollars, where they were welcome, where they could be themselves.

Trident had a lot of ups and downs during this time as well. We were not always the Golden Ship sailing high above the morals of common decency. We had some rough baristas, sold some sketchy books, and sometimes had to kick a few customers out for one reason or another. But we always came back to focusing on the coffee, the tea, the books, and the community. That formula seemed to work, and as kids who played in the sandbox on the back patio became dishers and eventually baristas, our community continued to grow and grow.

As Trident approached 30, it started to shift into legacy status. So many people have walked through the doors of Trident, have bought books here, have written books here, have found their first love (and maybe last love), and so on. The community reach of Trident had become international - friends of Trident live all across the United States, Europe, Australia, China, Ecuador, Mexico, Canada, and beyond. The Trident had become a "third space" that transcended time and place. It had become a sacred space.

The Daily Camera - June 24, 1992

NIGHT LINE: The art of hanging out is refined each evening at the Trident.

Photo by Eugene Tanner

"If you feel like you're being watched while seated at the Trident, you probably are... drink-balancing table-vultures frequently hover nearby."

CAFE BREAK

Cappuccino and camaraderie draw fans to Boulder's coffee houses

To see and be on the scene

The Trident, 940 Pearl St., isn't Boulder's oldest coffee house — it may not even be the biggest — but its wooden walls and floors and the attached bookstore make it one of the most well known. The loudest thing here is the buzz of voices. The crowd is mixed: Some come to read (magazines are hung on the wall, newspapers on a chest in the back room), some to write, some to talk... and talk. On weekends, tourists use their time in the winding line to get a close look at locals or scan the walls looking, in vain, for a list of drinks (menus are in a rack at the end of the counter). There is a touch of religious supplication in ordering drinks over the dark, high wooden counter. (Not wholly inappropriate, the word "cappuccino" is, after all, derived from a Capuchin monk's cowl.) As in any of Boulder's busier coffee houses, steely stares await the patron who has given no thought to an order prior to reaching the front of the line.

Espresso at the Trident is strong enough for the roasted flavor to come through and has a lively aftertaste, the cappuccino foam is on the creamy side. Regardless of the number of people waiting, the solo coffee maker maintains an even pace and does a good job of keeping the quality of the drinks up — no small feat when serving a line that never ends.

If you feel you're being watched while seated at the Trident, you probably are; there are rarely as many tables as patrons so drink-balancing table-vultures frequently hover nearby. Those willing to brave the sadistic spring on the front screen door can take advantage of a few tables out front that afford a nice view of motorists battling for parking on Pearl Street, bicyclists battling motorists, pedestrians dodging bicyclists and others who, lacking the ability or inclination to pass the evening quietly over coffee, busy themselves with the minutia of the world outside.

Article by Rob Fair

ESPRESSO BAR: When Trident Booksellers, off the Downtown Mall, added a coffee shop in 1983, owners just wanted to give readers a place to sit while they looked at books. Today, Trident is one of the old-timers in the Boulder coffee-house business.

The Daily Camera - September 10, 1991

Trident 1997

Explore the Pearl Street Pedestrian Mall, a vibrant historic preservation district that is Boulder's heart and soul. Enjoy one of Boulder's 300 sunny days at a sidewalk cafe—people watching and talented street performers add to the ambiance.

City of Boulder Brochure - 1999

BEST PLACE TO HAVE COFFEE

To sit, to sip, to dream: Boulder's most popular coffeehouse choice is no surpise. **Trident Booksellers, Inc.,** 940 Pearl St., manages to intrigue the tourists while keeping the locals in line for their daily grind.

Daily Camera - July 26, 1992

USA Today - March 8, 2002

10 great places for caffeine and conversation

Zoka Coffee Roaster and Tea Co.
Seattle

Folk, jazz and bluegrass performers add to the ambience at this Latteland (as Seattle is known) landmark, which boasts hardwood floors and couches for lounging. "Baristas don't think twice about throwing out a flawed espresso shot and trying again for perfection. That's why the espresso drinks, particularly the Americanos, are so sublime." 206-545-4277.

Stumptown Coffee Roasters
Portland, Ore.

Painstakingly prepared French-pressed coffee made from beans roasted on site is "to die for," but not the only lure at this 3-year-old cafe in southeast Portland. "Great music, an impressive magazine library and affordable art on the walls" round out the experience. 503-230-7797.

Trident Booksellers & Café
Boulder, Colo.

Grab a used book and sink your black-clad, beret-topped body into a chair to soak up the cerebral atmosphere. "The combination of coffee and literature welcomes conversation and relaxation. The menu is fairly simple, but the coffee, roasted by Freedom Coffee Roasters, is prepared with an eye on detail." 303-443-3133.

Intelligentsia Coffee Roasters & Tea Blenders
Chicago

Exposed ceilings and track lighting hover above a hodgepodge of wood tables and chairs at this Windy City institution, "known for sourcing some of the finest specialty coffees" — roasted locally in vintage German roasters. With an atmosphere at once "industrial and homey," it also offers superb teas served loose leaf in small pots. 773-348-8058.

"sink your black-clad, beret-topped body into a chair to soak up the cerebral atmosphere."

Best Espresso Bar of the 80's 90's and now!

The Daily Camera - February 19, 2004

Trident talk

Friendly Trident coffee klatch provides community for diverse group

Margie Sugar, left, and Karin Dremel Crouch chat during at the Trident Cafe on Pearl Street in Boulder, Crouch met her husband through the coffee group.

Article by: Susan Glairon

It is cold. Snow floats like feathers and sticks to hair like cotton candy. It's the kind of weather some cringe to drive in, others hate to walk through.

But still they come, by foot, by car, alone or with a friend.

They congregate along the east wall of Boulder's Trident Café, as they have for days and weeks and years.

They come for coffee and lattes, blueberry muffins and steaming tea, friendly greetings and boisterous conversations. It's a time to reconnect with old friends – most of whom they met at this very spot – and to indulge in chitchat and gossip. It's a time to be renewed with warm hugs and firm handshakes, with jokes and memories and plans of days to come.

The group, which has an email list of about 30, started roughly 17 years ago when several friends moved a coffee klatch from McDonald's on 28th Street to The Trident, says Jon Bond, 64, a retired IBM research programmer. Another part of the group originated at Fred's in the Boulderado Hotel in the 1950's, other members say.

Over the years some joined, others left. "I sat over there," says klatch member Karin Dremel Crouch, pointing to the west wall. "I looked at this group and thought, 'those people look so comfortable with eachother.'"

That was June 1997. She later married klatch regular Dee Crouch, a retired physician, also known known in Boulder for his sculptures.

At 47, Karin is one of the groups younger members. Ages vary from mid-40's through mid-70's, and their economic status ranges from modest to wealthy. Even their political stances swing from liberal to conservative.

They all have one thing in common. They want to connect.

"People that wouldn't have met under other circumstances have become really good friends," says Jane Ryland, 59, an education technology consultant.

The group often gets together for summer barbecues, Christmas parties and other social occasions, where attendance swells up to 50 with members' spouses.

At 7:40 a.m. on a recent Wednesday, Jon enjoys a cup of coffee while chatting with businesswomen Isle Gayle and Karin, a certified Rolfer.

Within 20 minutes, most of the tables lined across the east wall are filled with other members: Margie Sugar, 77, a homemaker and mother of four; Arthur Okner, 61, a retired New York businessman and Rebecca Jessup.

The conversation wanders; a recent party… serving in the armed forces in the 1960's… whether Margie should buy a new swimsuit for her trip to Mexico… Rebecca's son, who is learning Spanish in Mexico… Arthur's daughter, who is fluent in Spanish.

By 8:06, Jon is pouring another cup of coffee and Margie is munching a bran muffin. Margie's husband, who died in November, was also a regular.

"We just come here and enjoy each other," she says.

At 8:27 a.m., Phil Ecklund, a retired United pilot who also teaches an aviation class at Metro State, enters. Soon after, Margie leaves and Diane MacDonald, a retired Boulder judge, comes in, shaking Phil's hand.

"This is my secret love, but don't tell anyone," Phil says, a twinkle in his eye. Diane says she began coming to The Trident in 1982, when she worked as a public defender.

"I came here for years and drank my coffee and sort of got absorbed into this group," she says.

By 8:50, Jon is on his forth cup of decaffeinated coffee. At 8:52, Rick Kopp enters after a rough commute from Lafayette.

"I'm good, I'm late," says Rick, a self-disciplined "unemployed marketing genius".

By 8:58, Arthur is scrounging for quarters to help plug klatch members' parking meters. Parking is free until 9 a.m., the witching hour when most members usually leave because they don't want to pay. Today they decide to stay. As the newest member of the group, Arthur has the task of gathering quarters and feeding the meters.

Marc Weiss, 54, says he used to be a regular at the Carnival Café in Boulder, on Broadway between Canyon and Walnut. This klatch reminds him of those times.

"To me that was the old Boulder," Marc says. "There were cafes and coffeehouses. You would just meet people. You didn't have the isolation.

"Here (at the Trident) it kind of breaks that down. There is enough safety to talk to people. The Trident is the last vestige of that spirit when people were more open."

At 9:19, Jon says goodbye. According to other members, he's off to meet another group in another coffee shop.

"He's a serial monogamist coffee shop attendee," Rick jokes.

The others will hang out a little longer. This is their only stop.

"If I'm not here, people will ask, how I am, how I'm doing," Karin says. "It has become my community."

"The Trident is the last vestige of that spirit when people were more open."

Rebecca Jessup and Jon Bond laugh during their regular coffee klatch on a recent Wednesday morning at the Trident Cafe on Pearl St in Boulder.

Family Ties
by Rick Kopp

On November 14, 2012 this story was told to 150 people from the stage of the Melting Point in Athens, Georgia at Rabbit Box, a monthly storytelling event.

The Rabbit Box theme, this month, is "Family Ties." This story asks two questions: "What do you mean by family?" and, "What do you mean by ties?"

This true story of family ties happened in what urban planners call "The Third Place." The First Place is our home, where we typically expect to find family ties. The Second Place is our place of work, where we actually spend more time than we do at home. We also create ties with our work family.

Often, our home and work families seem to compete to see which one can be more dysfunctional. This drives us to seek refuge in The Third Place, which is a public gathering place. The pot belly stove of the old country store was a Third Place, as was the barbershop in some cultures. A "pub," being a contraction of "Public House," is a clear prototype of The Third Place.

For me, wherever I've lived, I've always had a Third Place: my coffee group family. I had one in New York. I had one in Atlanta. I had one in Boulder. And I have one here in Athens.

In Boulder, Colorado – where this story unfolded – my Third Place was the Trident Café. The Trident had high ceilings, raw brick walls, a wood stove in the back for snowy days, and – to be sure you knew exactly where you were – a large drawing of Jack Kerouac over the barista station as you entered.

The Trident had all the usual suspects: loners reading books; couples leaning into intimate conversations; and – a hallmark of a Third Place – "regulars," who, in the case of the Trident, ranged from young technology entrepreneurs to aging hippies.

Along the entire left wall, taking up all eight tables, was my large, animated coffee group. Crowded around each table were doctors, lawyers, artists, bankers, and more. I'd never seen anything like it before; and I haven't since. Overall, I spent two decades with my Trident family.

The full group, including spouses, met on Saturdays. On Wednesdays, there was a second gathering of a smaller subset of folks. But any day you'd go to the Trident, chances were good you'd run into someone you knew.

As people came in the front door and waited their turn to order their tea or latte or whatever, they'd be standing in line right next to our group. As a result, our group was known to everybody who came to the popular Trident Café. One time, around town, a stranger asked, "Don't I know you?" before having a realization and saying, "Oh, I know ... you're 'on the faculty' down at the Trident."

It was at the Trident that I met my longtime pal, Judge William H. Long, bon vivant, raconteur, and gourmet.

Bill had a look that didn't quite fit in Boulder. Boulder, you may know, is the healthiest city in the U.S. – lots of lean, wiry rock climbers in Spandex®. Bill didn't look like that. He was big. In fact, I liked sitting next to Bill so I'd be "the skinny guy". Bill loved to eat. Even more, he loved to cook.

Willy also dressed far less casually than most folks in Boulder. Being a Princeton grad, he had the collection of tweed jackets we folks from New England tend to assemble. He also enjoyed a broad array of interesting shirts. But Bill's trademark was the colorful butterfly that always fluttered at his throat, as if to underscore his ever-present smile. He had a huge collection of these.

When Judge Willy was on the bench in his judicial robe, the butterfly perched as though it had just emerged from a big black cocoon.

Our coffee group family – in addition to meeting at the Trident throughout the year – also had a summer party in Margie's beautiful garden and a winter party gathered around somebody's fireplace. At these social events, Judge Willy became Chef Willy, presiding over the main course. In place of his tweeds or robe was a huge tent of a white apron; and, peeking up from it, of course, the butterfly.

In the cruelest of ironies, our dear Bill – this great lover of food – was diagnosed with throat cancer. Gone was his butterfly; in its place, a ribbon of charred flesh, where the medieval methods of modern medicine had been applied to chase away the evil cancer spirits.

For a year, Bill got his nutrition through a feeding tube in his ever-shrinking belly. Finally, over a hundred pounds smaller, he emerged from his ordeal. They had to stretch his throat so he could eat solid food. But we had our cheerful Willy back with us.

Then, one day, they found Bill slumped over in his reading chair: dead from a heart attack. "Where," many of us asked, "was that serene exit back before his horrific year of torment?"

There was a memorial service for Bill. At the end of the event, Bill's lifelong friend, Betsy, stood at the front of the room. Next to her was a box containing Bill's extensive butterfly collection. A long line of folks waited patiently as, one by one, Betsy tied one of Willy's bowties around the throat of everyone on line. These are what I think of when I think of "Family Ties."

The Trident Faculty circa the early 90's

Evan Colbert Rules the Wasteland
by Evan Colbert

I worked at the Trident from 1990 to October 2001. They always said after 10 years that they would give you a pack of cigarettes and a revolver so you could end it the easy way. It turns out however that I was in my 11th year before I was mercifully taken on to the Trident afterlife. Back around 1992 I was enrolled in the photo programs at all three schools on the Auraria campus: CCD, UCD, and Metro. Community College of Denver actually had the most advanced program, and I was able to check out a 4x5 camera which I used to take these self-portraits at the Trident after closing time. We would close up shop with the help of a few beers, and once everyone else was gone I would commence taking photos of myself in various odd places, such as where the trash can would be in the dish washing area or on top of the refrigerator where the milk lived. It is amusing now to see that I captured the Trident in such minute and banal detail at such a specific moment of time. These photographs are literally antiques, almost 30 years old now.

Days of Beatitude

by Santiago Rodríguez Guerrero-Strachan

The poster of the conference on Jack Kerouac was hanging on the wall behind the counter of the café where I had stopped by to have a coffee on a dull, chilling evening, or so it seems to me now. That was in 1994. I had arrived in Boulder a week before for a short-term stay at the University and I still ignored the close relation of the Beats and Boulder. On my first Friday, I went downtown in the afternoon just to 'explore' the city. I rambled up and down Pearl Street, a street full of life and flowers even at such a late time in the year. After some half an hour watching the people, the shops and the restaurants, I walked West beyond Broadway. I came across a large shop window that displayed several rows of books, most of them used, I noticed later. There was something in it, maybe the light inside or the few people talking, that made me enter. Several bookcases covered the walls and filled the room. I browsed the shelves just out of curiosity to get an idea about the kind of bookshop it was. I still remember the books on nature, on Oriental religions, a few others were presidential biographies and, farther into the library, a whole bookcase with poetry. I would buy two or three, I cannot remember now, maybe Robert Lowell's Life Studies, and Allen Ginsberg's essays.

    I was by the counter, when I saw another room, so I asked the woman about it. I was welcome to come into the café and have a coffee or a tea, if you please. At first, I was surprised for the silent atmosphere of the place and for the strong smell of coffee. In the large room, divided in two, there were people sitting at the tables, talking quietly and a queue of other people waiting to have their coffees served. I was not used to this as in Spain you ordered your coffee when you were sitting at a table, but it mattered little to queue for my coffee. While waiting, and after having read the drinks menu several times, I saw behind the bar, on the wall opposite the entry door, the poster of Jack Kerouac.

There he was, the writer I had read too young and who maybe had inspired me to study American literature. It might be chance or it might be fate. I still do not know, but something changed in my life, not radically or dramatically, but rather smoothly, as changes have always been. I would spend most of my evenings in the café. Some days I had a café florentine, but most of the days I had regular coffee. I still remember that I ordered one and had a free refill. Subsequent refills cost only 35 cents, as I read in a note. I bought Barry Miles's biography of Kerouac and sat at the back of the place in the evenings. I spent quite a lot of time reading, but since I was a quiet presence that passed unnoticed, I also watched the people who entered and sat in front of me or at the next table. I talked very little to the people there, but I still remember a young man with a black cap who spent a few hours with a coffee while he jotted down notes in a black notebook, and the young women who sat in the armchairs to talk always in a hushed voice. A few Sunday mornings I had breakfast there. I would find a table near the door in the corner by the counter. The winter sun light entered to make the coffee in the cup shine. I loved that spot since I could observe the many regular costumers ordering their Sunday morning coffees and cinnamon rolls, the talks they had while waiting and the kind words of goodbye they said to the baristas, in particular to a quiet man who moved from the rear of the bookshop to the counter bringing bags of coffee. Some time later I learned he was Mike, the owner.

Only years later I realized those were my days of beatitude.

EM & EM

by Emily Owens and Emma Gomis

Dear Emily,

It's hard to write about things that make us sentimental, about things that make us feel nostalgic; yet maybe these are some of the most important things to write about, our formative experiences. I'm so glad that you found this poem we wrote together so many years ago and sent it over. Reading it, I was overwhelmed with details I hadn't conjured in years. The first impressions of the Trident: the curtains in the windows, the cigarettes we shared out back in the parking lot, the conversations at the tables (or, when we were lucky enough, one of the booths with the maroon benches), passing books back and forth and quoting Richard Brautigan, the art on the walls, the boys we crushed on, the chocolate pumpkin bread and black coffee. We became friends when I printed out a photograph of Carson McCullers and wrote you a note on the back saying that the photograph was how I pictured you in your old age. I was sixteen, you were a year older. I was so nervous when I brought it to you in the back room of the Trident, my coffee spilling out of the cup and onto the saucer, but you laughed and asked me to sit down. We wrote poems, sitting at those tables, nodding to all the regulars, letting our imaginations bloom in a collaboration that only that space could foster. Our lives were there, the only social outlet in what felt, to us, like a small town. Still now, when I go into the Trident, I feel the traces of those days, the excitement and complicity in discovering that we were poets. Now so many years later, after completing my MFA in Creative Writing & Poetics at Naropa and about to start a PhD in Literature at the University of Cambridge, I still think it was there, in that space, among the books and coffee, that I fell in love with poems. Do those days hold the same kind of weight in you?

Yours,

Emma

Emma,

My dear old friend, you are the poet! I have since retired, never to return, into the delightful misery of art criticism.

You can only imagine the sadness I felt now, spending hours in search for the letter which sealed our friendship. I have torn apart my house, skimming through each and every notebook of my youth, through stacks of papers and memories, souvenirs of the past, with it nowhere to be found. Painful, as I know that it is here (hiding in a book no doubt), as I ran into it only a couple of months ago. Alas, it resides in my memory as much of that time does. I was able to find some other artifacts, which may be of interest to you, and the Trident alike and they can be found at the end of this letter.

I began my tenure at the Trident in 1995. My mother and I spent our time between the Penny Lane Coffeehouse (gone now) and the Trident for much of my youth. When the Penny Lane closed in 2007, my next decade was spent entirely within the walls of the Trident. Mike Smith, was my emotionally surrogate father. Anne and Allen, my mentors. The pencil sharpener, which hangs at the threshold between the bookstore and the cafe, a sort of totem that followed me throughout my youth. As I became older, it remained, a staple of my memory. I fell in love for the first time, in its walls, forbiddingly, with a barista who worked there. I made my closest friends, and spent hours upon countless hours lost within poems and novels and learning to write my own. I learned how to be a human through the teachings of my lost, but never really lost, friend Erik Winn (a friend to us all), for whom Mike Smith helped me to arrange a small memorial on the very back patio I had spent years unknown to death. I had small beginnings as a detective, at the ripe age of nine years old, when I would spy on Boris and Peggy, and write down their every move as if some great drama were about to unfold. I met you. And you and I learned to craft ourselves as poets through constant questions as young students of literature, philosophy, and poetry. We plummeted, pummelled, sometimes outright impaling ourselves on the very notions of existence itself as we ran headstrong into our youth, searching for beauty in every nook and cranny of the small, comfortable walls of the Trident which contained us, and all that was to be found outside of us. Its smell still sticks to my coat. Its taste still lingers on my tongue. I am so glad to hear of you, my friend, and how well you are doing and where you are going, and to know that the great anniversary of my most cherished cafe is amongst us. Long live the Trident, may it always be a home to every walk of life!

-Emily Owens

Photo taken in front of the Trident circa 2006 when we met

EINSTEIN'S EQUILIBRIUM

By Emily Owens and Emma Gomis
(written at the Trident in 2006)

Einstein's equilibrium's on the shelf
His cranial apparatus on the one below
But this is not an ordinary library
Filled with books and musty lights
Small children with large framed glasses
Passing their time
Staring at old war pictures of Gandhi

"The only part we couldn't understand,"
Said the Jury
"Were the light bulb
Placed in cans and jars
Filled with molasses– and illuminating the shattered glass
rims"

Ulysses last parade brings a crowd of
Black suited creatures
To aisles I through M
Joyce's Irish lungs quiver from the 3rd
Book on the 2nd shelf
Shakespeare is alone
Feeling neglected and despondent

And-

From the corner of the room
Small clay speakers said
"The books, the books spoke to me!
They have nothing to say"

And from the opposite side of the room
Someone began to shout
"There's too much going on here"
It was the reader
Their small face radiating with feverish content
And the writer paused

Lifted fingers from typewriter
Shuffled a moment
Mounted a cardboard box
And directed
Mozart's second opera
With various forms of
Plastic cutlery

Cigarette ashes have covered his struggling manuscript and the
Literary customers are blinded by another dramatic pause -

The librarian has crawled under the couch
Sniffing barbed wire
And drinking instant coffee

The readers, by now overwhelmed with the chaotic tumult
Have run off to the nearest prison
Where the images are less complex
They see
Guards and last meals
Imprisonment and despair

And by god,
We all know those things are simple

"But on with the story!"
The writer decides,
Though deciding is too easy
She does no such thing.
It's not a matter of intensity
Of actions
Of stepping off the stiff brown paper
And going back to the story…
But much to his despair,
The readers having found bland predictable boredom,
Had already returned to their homes where small dusty chandeliers

Illuminate the invisible

The Trident Cafe: A Writer's Manifesto
by Jenn Zuko

(Written in 2000; revised in 2006)

"Isak Dinesen said that she wrote a little every day, without hope and without despair. Someday I'll put that on a three-by-five card and tape it to the wall beside my desk." ~Raymond Carver

The Trident Cafe here in Boulder, Colorado has a number of spells that hover over it and in its interior air. Situated between a Tibetan gift shop and Jax Fish House, it serves both the best coffee in Boulder and used books and remainders of all kinds.

Walk with me through the bright coolth of a Boulder Spring day (oops, hold your nose: a crew of dreadlocked wookiies (1) are walking by...whew okay that's over)...there's Rhumba, nope can't write anything in there. Why? Well, their rum list is the size of a fancy restaurant's wine list, so we'll wait till later for that.

As we enter the Trident, we should keep our eyes vulture-peeled for an available seat. Notice the wood throughout: wood floors, wood and brick walls, wooden bar, wood-grain tables, dark wood and leather chairs...if there was ever a fire in here (God forbid) you could steep the ashes in water for espresso. Be thinking about what you want to drink as the artistically-dressed young bussers flutter around us. There are two Naropa students, one Pearl Street Mall employee with a list for her office, and two yuppies (2) in line ahead of us, so we have time to think about our beverage choice. Check out the wall of labeled exotic teas behind the tattooed barista. You bet your orange pekoe he can tell you about every one of them, never mind his apparent youth and bold ink. Go ahead, ask.

Good choice: that tea will literally bloom into little jasmine blossoms in the water. I'll order my usual (I often don't even have to order anymore): a Florentine. Poor man's mocha. Strong bitter coffee and hot chocolate. Still can't make 'em like that at home.

All the best (and published) writing I have ever done has been at the Trident. Not without exception, but pretty much. I have been frequenting this place since teenager-hood with my blank books, and I feel after a good solid hour longhand there I have actually gotten more work done than I could at home with a parrot on my shoulder or at any computer. I am a big believer in the benefits of caffeine as a "happy drug," conducive to my writing flow and brain waves. Maybe that's the only magic spell the Trident needs--the coffee seeped into the wood (and bricks) surrounding me. They also have art exhibits on the walls, which is always a good thing, even if the art is not. Writing and art go hand in hand, even in my journals, and it behooves me to have artwork around. The bustle of people and music in the cafe doesn't distract me, in fact, if I ever hit a brick wall, I start Found Conversation until it goes away.

What does interrupt me is my own self (just count the number of parentheses in this informal piece of writing and you'll see what I mean). If I decide to write at home, there are always a thousand things to do instead: play with the parrot or cat, grade papers, surf the 'Net, play a computer game, rotate laundry or dishes, watch the Food Network, drink a beer, hang out with my husband, play a computer game, do Tai Chi...not always necessarily bad for me, but certainly bad for my writing.

Back in the day, I had an acting professor corner me and demand I do a production he'd been working on called A Room of One's Own, based on the Virginia Woolf piece and a performance by a well-known Dame of the RSC (3). I never ended up doing it, but researched it till it fell through (4). In the piece, Woolf says it's important to work in a room of one's own, precisely for the above reasons. That was the main lesson I got from that research: that you have to make writing the most important thing happening for a certain hour on a certain day, no matter how many checks have bounced or how many people are crying (or dying) in the world. For what work do I really have to do, besides write? Later, a well-known poetry prof (Linda Hogan, in fact) said the same thing: "Turn the phone off," she'd say, "because, you know, it may be somebody handsome calling.." (5) No distraction is as important as the writing at hand. Doing it is so much more important than the quality of actual stuff produced.

Example: a poem that came out one day at the Trident was sent out with no revision whatsoever, I barely even remember having written it--that half-asleep state that comes with a caffeine crash--and it was my first published piece.

Okay, I'm not advocating non-revision, that's ridiculous, I'm just saying that there's something about dropping everything and going to the Trident for an hour or two that makes my writing what it is.

What is it? Sword-and-sorcery, or just sword, or just sorcery. Or Holmesian mystery. Or all three? I have a terrible habit of dipping into the collective unconscious at the wrong time, without banking on it quickly enough. Examples? I had young people going to wizard's school (inspired by LeGuin's Roke) back in the '80s when I was going to junior high and high school with a bad knee. My Wizards' school was a gym class substitute (of course, LeGuin and McKinley did it before I was born, but). Now that Harry Potter has a worldwide following, I wonder why I never finished my own tale. I worked closely with Jenny Heath on my sprawling pirate epic: five long stories in a fantasy world resembling our own Golden Age of pirates (mid to late 1700s Europe), researched joyfully and diligently, reworked and reconsidered, and even begun transformation into a comic book script at the advice of an artist friend in the trade. And after a half-chapter was ready for the penciller, what comes out on the market? A comic series called El Cazador. With a spunky lady pirate, and a red-headed adversary/love interest...all beautifully drawn...a bestseller...oh and don't even get me started on the sexy vampires, I've got some sexy vampires (no they don't fucking sparkle)...

There is a character from old school Sesame Street named Don Music. He had nerdy glasses and a sloppy mop of grayish hair. He'd always be sitting at his piano, trying to compose nursery rhymes. He would never quite get them right ("Mary had a bicycle...") but he'd keep trying and trying until finally he'd exclaim: "I'll never get it, never, never!!!" And he'd whack his head onto the piano and sob. I seem to have Don Music moments often, when I'm nearly done with a second or third draft of something and am scouting around for potential markets. But oh well, I'll be at the next nursery rhyme in the next episode, without fail...

I find the Old Stories to be the most important--I force them upon any students I happen to have, no matter what the subject. Folks, especially younger folks, don't know the old tales well enough--I mean, put them in the Forbidden Forest and they wouldn't know to give that old weird beggar their food; or not to eat or drink anything a fairy gives them, or to offer to work to get into the magic palace...things any human should know well.

So my writing is recycled archetype. I think I'm okay with that.

----

(1) Wookiies are rich white young people who sport dreadlocks and a myriad other Hipster inclinations.
(2) Yuppies are hippies who grew up to be very high financed businesspeople.
(3) Eileen Atkins
(4) my writing and my acting have always been trained in tandem, but not necessarily together until recently. My life of education has been tending the earth of two separate trees--now they've grown close enough together as to share vines and branches, if not roots.
(5) this was uttered during a graduate poetry class, it must have been in 1995? CU Boulder.

Legacies Never Die

Over the last decade, Trident has continued its pursuit of excellence. Just because we have been operating for 40 years does not mean we are no longer pursuing excellence. In fact, our community demands it of us!

To that end, we have continued to improve our coffee and tea program, we have expanded and improved our book selection, and we even started our own publishing house. Aiming for excellence does not mean "buying the most expensive," but rather finding partners who share our same ideals and goals. Often that means working directly with producers to make sure money and capital are shared equitably across the supply chain.

Campos Coffee is our friend, partner, and coffee roaster. Over the past 12 years they have worked tirelessly to bring "quality coffee cultivated by good" to your cup. Forming long-term relationships directly with farmers has allowed them to not only buy some of the best coffees in the world, but to provide farmers with a direct and guaranteed income year after year. Campos continuously strives for excellence, just like we do. Together, our larger community reaps the benefits - superior coffee, an equitable supply chain, meaningful relationships, and environmental stewardship.

Our tea program has mirrored our coffee program. We have made big steps in building direct relationships with tea farmers in China, India, and Taiwan, and we can now proudly claim that all of our tea comes direct from the farm. With over 200 teas offered each year, it has been a long journey to build and foster our larger community to include tea growers and producers. Again, this has allowed us to build healthy, equitable, long term relationships directly with the farmers and producers, resulting in some of the best teas in the entire Rocky Mountain region being offered. We are the only cafe in the region that works directly with farmers and producers, and the results are easy to taste.

Finally, we have continued to invest in the bookstore, doubling down on our commitment to the community to provide a wide range of books across all spectrum's of beliefs and opinions. Knowledge is power, and our community is one of the brightest, most alive, knowledge seeking communities - and we are honored to be able to continue that path towards excellence by offering a wide selection of new and used books.

Driving towards excellence is how we never let the legacy of Trident die. Excellence demands a multi-pronged approach, and the Trident Booksellers and Café being a trident, is exactly how we have continued towards that goal - coffee, tea, and books. Those three prongs of Trident have built the community that we are honored to support today, and our commitment to excellence means we will continue that three pronged approach into the future.

We demand it. Our community demands it. Our legacy demands it.

Photos by
Mark Kodak

October 2018
by Chet Ananda

My daughter Bekah and I were showing Aish, her boyfriend from India, Boulder's Pearl Street Mall. This was his first trip to Colorado. Back when Bekah was a kid after her mom and I divorced, she and her brother would visit me in the summer. I worked downtown on Walnut in 1982 and she remembered walking through the Trident to get pitas across the street. On the way back we would stop at the coffeehouse for drinks. Amazingly enough, the Trident is still in existence and looking much the same as it did forty years ago when many of us hippies were evolving into spiritual seekers studying eastern traditions.

Bekah, Aish, and I, after strolling down the mall, ended up having beers, nachos, and laughs in a brew pub which had once been the location of the long-gone pita shop, Johnny Pirates. "Boulder was different then—not so much up-scale," noted Bekah.

"Back then, Aish, Boulder was like a spiritual supermarket—Yogis, Sufis, Zen monks, Jesus Freaks, Tibetan Buddhists, Rajneeshees, Sikhs were offering classes and lectures on all things enlightening!"

"I don't believe in religions," Aish said.

"Neither did we--we thought these ideas were new," I indicated.

"It was a cultural revolution for the baby-boomers," Bekah interjected, "They were trying to escape their parents' beliefs."

"Actually, awesomeness is my religion," Aish said, smiling.

Artwork: Mahalia Mae Porter

Trident Regulars
by Ben Rietema

I am a regular at the Trident. Some may wonder if I ever really leave, or if I sleep in the basement and then emerge the next morning, like a benevolent ghost that drinks too much caffeine.

Am I homeless or is it just that I never go home? It's hard to tell, but when I'm passed out in the back corner with my nest of backpacks and clothing and papers and crystals and I'm sporting the long hair and beard of an underground communist and I'm babbling about things that no one understands... well, it's still impossible to tell whether I'm a Naropa student or homeless.

Sometimes I talk about socialism. Sometimes I talk about conservatism. Sometimes I talk about astrology. Sometimes I talk about some really weird shit. And all this conversation combines with music to form a warm hum that reminds me of everything that is right with everything.

In the winter, I appreciate the warmth and serenity of being packed in with fifty other people who don't have a normal job. The wood stove is burning, and if I am sitting directly next to it, I am required to strip down to my underwear in order to avoid losing half my body weight in sweat. I watch new people come and choose this seat, and I see how long it takes before they break down and start crying.

In the summer, I appreciate the space and the courtyard and the nights where I can watch an indie movie that is both weird and incredibly compelling. Then, I stumble home in the dark, feeling happy but also wondering what I just watched.

Art is often hung around the walls of the Trident, and I appreciate this art, even if it's paintings of people and I feel like they're staring at me. Like a whole room of people who are staring at me. Without blinking.

Every once in a while, I attend a reading for writers who are desperate to receive validation, like a teenager that wears the same overlarge sweatshirt during the day and cries alone at night. They are passionate in ways that only artists who ascend to the tantalizing highs of creative work and then fall to the crushing lows of reality are.

Their work is often confusing and filled with metaphors, depression, strange humor, mushroom trips, and references to sexual experiences that I didn't know were possible. I laugh. I cry. I am proud to be a part of a community that values these heart-broken, poverty-stricken creators.

I have been ordering the same drink for years. Rarely will I even look at the other items I can order at the Trident, whether that is a vivid green hippie drink or a CBD-infused sense of unreality.

If my order changes, the barista may ask if I'm doing okay and give me the number for a crisis line. And I will take that number, call, and spend a few hours explaining the drastic life circumstances that have caused me to switch to a drink with slightly more foam.

It is these Trident employees—Crystal, Wysteria, Jake, Nate, Liz, and all the rest—who function as a foundation for my life. I depend on them to be there. They are never allowed not to be working at the Trident. They must die here simply because I really like these people. And I cannot handle change.

When I meet other regulars outside of the Trident, I talk about any changes that may have occurred to the coffee shop, like an automatic paper towel dispenser, a bench, or new soap. And this affirms our common bond, even if it's drinking beverages in the same place and commenting about super boring things.

Trident Press: The First Three Years
by Nathaniel Kennon Perkins

It was Trident that brought me back to Boulder, CO.

I'd spent some time in this city previously, living in a radical housing co-op with 15 other people and working a variety of odd jobs, but my aimlessness had left me dissatisfied, and I'd packed up and split town before even being here a year. New Mexico was next. I posted up in the mountains outside of Albuquerque and tried to get a community living homestead project off the ground.

It failed miserably.

Heart heavy, I headed back north to stay with my sister in Colorado Springs. I had to figure out what I was going to do with my life. There didn't seem to be many good options. But it was during this time that I reached out to some Boulder friends and drove up to visit. A few of them had just moved into a new house and had an open bedroom I could rent. I was dead broke, and I remembered well the extortionate expense of Boulder rents, but I said I'd consider it. Next, I visited my friend and former housemate Stela Knezevic, who at that time was working on the bookstore side of Trident. She told me that another employee had just quit, and there was a position open. Did I want to apply for the job? And just like that, Boulder, a place I had mistakenly added to my personal list of failures, pulled me back in.

My first training shift at Trident was in February of 2017. I started out as a disher, like everyone does. However, my extremely nerdy love of books, especially small press literary fiction, motivated me to move over to the bookstore side of the operation as quickly as possible. I didn't have any retail experience to speak of, but I loved being surrounded by literature and the people who appreciated it. I'd always dreamt of working in a bookstore, and I tried to do a good job.

After a few months, Peter Jones, the general manager, came to me with a proposal:

"How would you feel about starting and running a publishing house based out of Trident?"

Another of my dreams come true. At that time, I was reading everything I could get my hands on by independent publishing houses like Pioneers Press, Lazy Fascist, and House of Vlad. I felt invigorated and inspired by them for the same reason I've always liked punk music and DIY culture. People were creating poignant, beautiful art outside of the prescribed and alienating mainstream channels. They were making it happen, taking everything into their own hands, tradition be damned. But I didn't want to just be a consumer; I wanted to be an active contributor to the artistic and literary movement.

So I said yes.

Then I took stock of my non-existent experience and resources.

What the hell were we going to publish?

I reached out first to my friend Noah Cicero, the poet and novelist. We'd met a few years earlier, right after the release of his poetry collection Bipolar Cowboy, when I'd helped set up a reading for him at The King's English bookstore in Salt Lake City, where I was living at the time. We had stayed in touch over the years, so I knew he'd been sitting on a manuscript. It was a philosophical non-fiction book about Buddhism. Because this was something so apart from the writing he was known for, he'd been having a hard time finding a publisher. Without ever having seen a page of it, I offered to publish it through Trident Press. Noah trusted me, and in November of 2017—with the help of cover artist Rachel Pfeffer—we put out the first Trident Press book: Blood-Soaked Buddha, Hard Earth Pascal.

The next two books were also written by literary friends. I reached out to Jasper Avery and Katie Foster, both incredible poets, both enrolled in MFA writing programs on the East Coast at that time. Jasper's book, it gets cold, was about queer identity and space. Mallory Whitten, another of my favorite contemporary poets, did the cover art. Katie's book, Major Diamonds Nights & Knives, was based on the tarot and written while the author felt as though she was possessed by a ghost that had died during childbirth. Really cool stuff.

Feeling as though a pretty solid foundation had been laid, I published my own book next. Cactus, a short novel, was my first full-length work. It came out in March of 2018. I followed that pretty quickly with a collection of some of the shorter writings of the turn-of-the-century anarcho-communist philosopher Peter Kropotkin. My idea was to create a radically political book that someone could keep in their pocket and sneakily read at work while they were supposed to be doing something else. I called it, of course, The Pocket Peter Kropotkin.

The fifth book marked the end of what I consider to be the first wave of Trident Press. This was Sixty Tattoos I Secretly Gave Myself at Work by Tanner Ballengee. Tanner was someone I'd become friends with through the internet and later in real life when I took a solo road trip to Arizona, where he lives. He was a zine writer and a skateboarder and a punk. Sixty Tattoos was just what it sounded like: The stories about and behind a bunch of stick-and-poke tattoos the author had furtively given himself while on the clock at a call center. It immediately got a positive review in Thrasher Magazine and shot to the top of some of Amazon's bestseller lists.

Armed with these five titles, I spent almost three weeks in the summer of 2018 touring around the country with the Kansas City-based emo band, Tall Boys. I gave a reading from Cactus every night, they played songs off their new album, and afterwards I sold Trident Press books. I'd had a bunch of Trident Press stickers printed up, and I stuck them everywhere we went: venues, bars, truck stops, public bathrooms. I was determined to get the word out.

Another book in the pocket series came next, The Pocket Emma Goldman. Goldman was a contemporary of Kropotkin's, an accessible and funny writer, and hero of mine. This book collected many of her shorter works.

Then another heavy hitter: A novel called The Silence is the Noise by Bart Schaneman. I'd been a huge fan of Bart's writing for a long time, so when he sent me this manuscript about a small-town newspaper reporter covering the story of a fracking wastewater injection operation that was causing earthquakes, I said yes immediately. This novel is so true to Bart's voice and his body of work. Its heart is purely American, and it explores what it means to be shaped by the places we're from. While I love every book that Trident Press has put out, The Silence is the Noise is objectively one of the best of them. Plus, it has a great cover by the painter and designer Marsha Robinson.

This is when Jake Dirnberger, Trident's assistant manager, jumped on board, bringing with him a background in Western philosophy and the occult. He edited and wrote the introduction for The Pocket Aleister Crowley, which helped the pocket series keep from focusing exclusively on leftist politics. Of course, I did my best to shift the balance back again by editing and releasing The Soul of Man Under Socialism by Oscar Wilde and Propaganda of the Deed: The Pocket Alexander Berkman.

Meanwhile, my second book, a collection of short stories called The Way Cities Feel to Us Now, had come out from a Chicago-based publisher called Maudlin House. I went on tour again in the summer of 2019, this time with the writer, publisher, and musician Adam Gnade. The car's suspension was maxed out from the weight of all those books, but after a couple weeks and a couple thousand miles, we'd managed to sell most of them. It felt good. Things were going in the right direction.

When I got back, a bunch of projects started happening all at once. Jake Dirnberger was working on editing another occult book. Taylor Sumner, fellow bookstore clerk and literary nerd, wanted to become more involved with the press, and she suggested that we open to submissions. I was more than happy to let these two capable folks take the lead on those endeavors. I was busy editing and laying out Los Espíritus by Josh Hyde. Josh, a filmmaker and podcaster, was a regular customer at Trident. I was familiar with his work, and I loved it. Los Espíritus was somewhat experimental in form for Trident Press. It was a screenplay, something we'd never put out before, and it was a challenge, but a lot of fun.

Jake finished The Pocket Austin Osman Spare, which collects much of the writings and art of the "Godfather of Chaos Magick." It was super bizarre, sometimes disturbing, but 100% fascinating stuff. Taylor accepted two submitted poetry manuscripts: America at Play by Mathias Svalina and Western Erotica Ho by Bram Riddlebarger. America at Play is a collection of rules for surreal children's games, and is as bizarre and cool as you'd expect anything from Svalina, someone who runs a "Dream Delivery Service," to be. It came out in March of 2020. Western Erotica Ho was released in July of 2020.

In the beginning of 2020, I also got a pitch from the fiction writer Nick Gregorio. I'd followed Nick's work for a couple years, and I loved the two books he'd written, a novel and a story collection. But what he was sending me now was something entirely different. The book, With a Difference, had been inspired by the 2002 Rancid/NOFX split album from BYO Records, on which each band covered the other's songs. Nick, along with the poet Francis Daulerio, had taken this concept a step further. Francis had turned ten of Nick's stories into poems, and Nick had adapted ten of Fran's poems into stories. The book would have two front covers, meaning that it would be flipped over like a record to be fully experienced. I said yes almost immediately. The book came out May of 2020.

In three years, Trident Press has put out 16 books. It's been an insane amount of work, especially considering I didn't know how to do any of it when I started. Acquisitions, editing, design, sales, distribution, etc. But it's also been extremely fulfilling. I've gotten to go to conferences, host readings, and table at zine and literary festivals. I've met so many amazing people through running

Trident Press. My life is completely different than if Peter hadn't asked me to do it. Moving back to Boulder was the best decision I've ever made.

And I feel like we're actively contributing to the literary community. It's been great to run the press out of the bookstore because it means we have built-in sales and a built-in audience, but Trident Press's reach extends much further than that. Trident Press orders have shipped to almost every continent. Bookstores, skate shops, and record stores across the country stock our titles.

One time, the poet Anne Waldman walked into the bookstore. Admittedly, I was a little star struck. As she was headed out the door, I awkwardly handed her a stack of Trident Press books and told her a little bit about the project.

She said, "I've been waiting thirty years for Trident to do this."

It feels good.

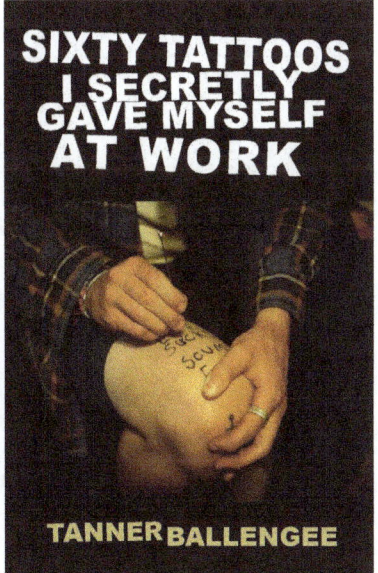

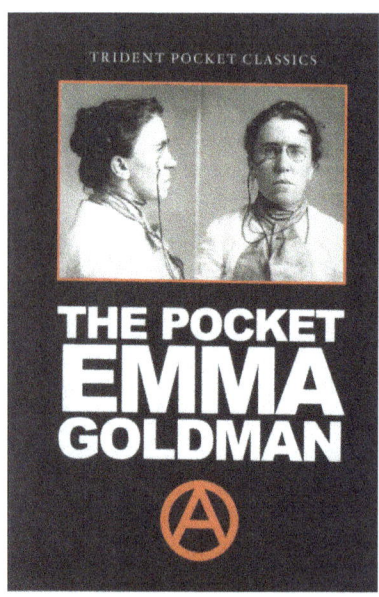

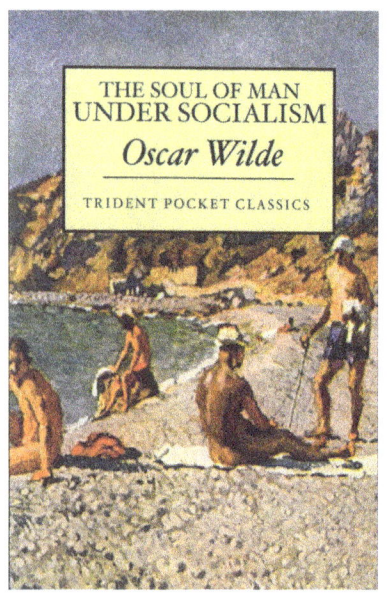

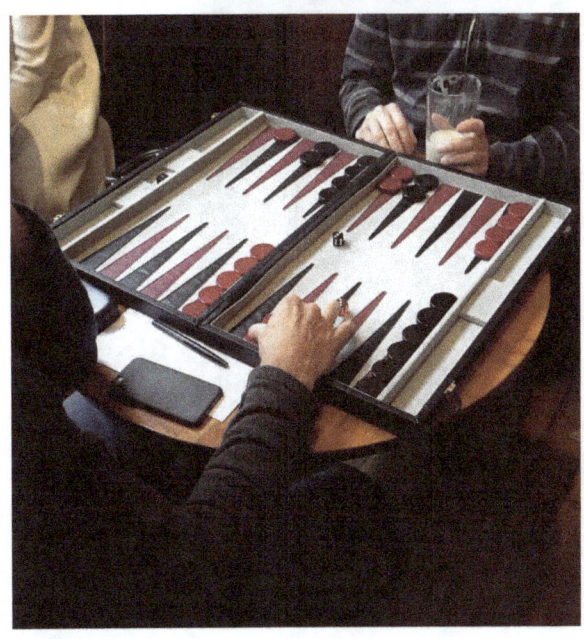

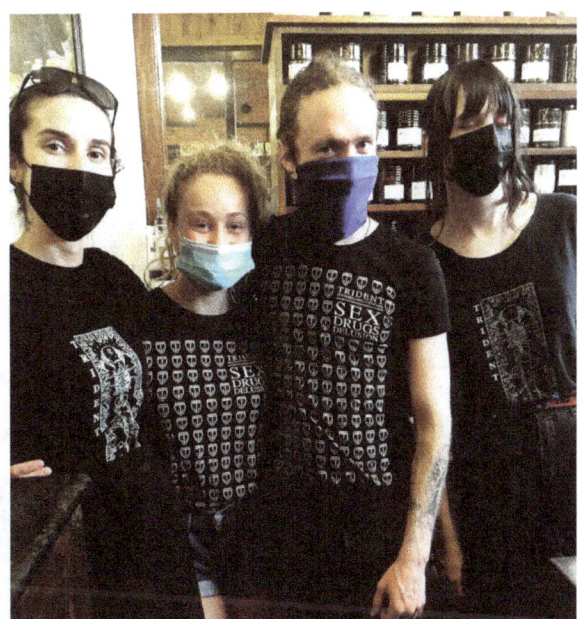

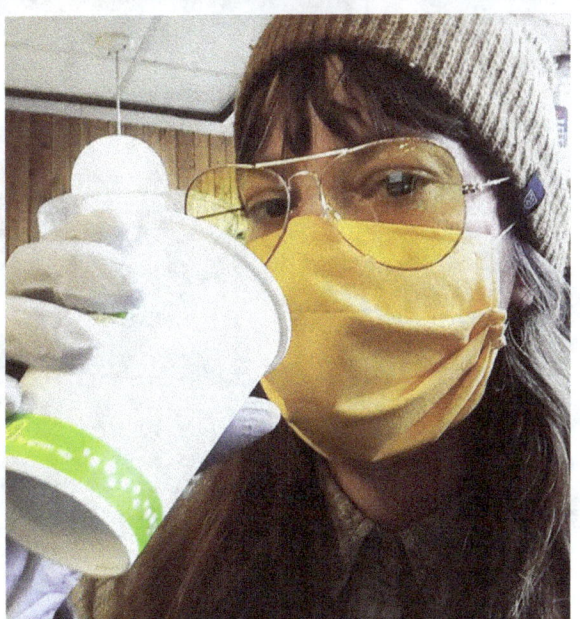

The Next Chapter

After 40 years of serving the community, Trident looked inward and decided to serve its staff. In September eight longtime employees signed their names on the bottom line as the Trident became employee-owned for the first time.

The new Trident partnership group from left to right: Ashkan Angha, Scott Raderstorf, Jake Dirnberger, Peter Jones, Sara Preinitz, Dillon Cramer, Joellen Raderstorf, Sofia Miranda, Cyanne Stonesmith, Wysteria Bristol, Crystal Garcia. (Not pictured: Amanda Angha)

"As in most small businesses, there was always tension between the owners and employees," notes longtime employee and General Manager Peter Jones. "We wanted to eliminate that tension and make everyone an equal contributor to the success of the Trident. Now everyone pulls their own weight and the Trident can move forward without many of the traditional roadblocks one finds when employees work for owners."

"I love my work and the community at the Trident," said Crystal Garcia on the night of the ownership signing. "If I thought about doing anything else, it would be to open another coffee shop just like the Trident somewhere else. Now I am an owner." Although managing the bottom line and paying the rent is essential in this unprecedented time, Cyanne Stonesmith, a new partner, makes it clear that the Trident's success owes to the fact that "we value people and the community over profits, and we will continue to do so."

"Everyone belongs at the Trident—everyone," says Ashkan Angha, an owner for 14 years.

The Trident partnership team is excited about this new turn for the Trident, and we look forward to serving the community for another 40 years!

Dedications

This book is dedicated to all the members of the Trident family that are no longer with us. The following list of departed was compiled by Erika Rice.

Richard Arthure, "Kunga Dawa": Secretary to Trungpa Rinpoche
Joe Bankhead: Lived in his camper
Harlan Barton: Rode on tramp steamers, produced hiking maps
Janis Belliponti
Fritz Clausen
Carol Crutchlow
Sharon Dunham
Randi Eyre
Tom Finley: "Yah-te-hey! Live Long and Prosper!"
Mel Holzman
Ted Howard
Gene Levine
George Lichter
Bill Long
Adam Rubenstein: "Every day is a gift"
Harold Rydstedt
Ellen Sears
Clark Southard: "Better to be seen than viewed!"
Margie Sugar
George Sugar
Mike True, "Caballa Blanca": Long-distance runner